LITTLE LIBRARY

Guide to
Spain

Jackie Gaff

Kingfisher Books

NEW YORK

Contents

Welcome to Spain

A family of tourists unpacks their car in a sunny Spanish village. Brilliant red geraniums hang from the balconies of whitewashed houses. The vacation stretches ahead — long, hot days for swimming along beautiful, sandy beaches, trips inland to explore wild forests and pretty, hilltop villages, or visits to one of Spain's many fascinating and ancient cities.

Spain and its islands

Mainland Spain is in the southwestern corner of Europe, almost surrounded by sea. Also part of Spain are the Balearic Islands and far to the south, near the coast of Africa, the Canary Islands.

A vast plain covers the center of Spain, much of it farming land. It is broken by mountain ranges, some so high that people ski on them in winter.

SPANISH MONEY

In Spain, the money people use is called pesetas. When you go to a bank, you'll see signs that show you how much Spanish money you can get in exchange for your own money.

ATLANTIC
OCEAN

France

SPAIN

Portugal

Madrid

R.Ebro

Barcelona

Valencia

Balearics

R. Guadalquivir

Seville

MEDITERRANEAN
SEA

AFRICA

In a Spanish town

I n the center of most small towns and villages you'll find a *plaza* (main square), lined with stores and cafés.

Spain has long been a Catholic country and to one side of the *plaza*, there is often a church.

1. *Cerámicas* – store selling local pottery
2. *Ultramarinos* – grocery store
3. *Farmacia* – drugstore
4. *Panadería* – bakery   5. Banco – bank
6. *Oficina de Correos* – post office

FRESH FISH

Spain is famous for its wonderful fresh seafood. At the *pescadería* (fish store), look out for *boquerones* (whitebait) — these tiny fish are often fried and eaten whole. *Calamares* (squid) are also very tasty.

Life slows down in the heat of the day. Stores usually shut at lunchtime, while people eat or take a *siesta* (a nap). Places open up again in the late afternoon, finally closing at 8 P.M. or later.

9

Going shopping

V isiting a bustling street market is one of the best ways to discover what the Spanish like to eat and drink. Here you'll find piles of fresh fruit and vegetables and tubs of shining olives. Some stalls display different sausages, others sell nothing but *queso* (cheese). Best of all, perhaps, are the stalls selling the thin curly doughnuts called *churros*.

You'll find souvenir shops in most towns. Popular gifts are fans, pottery, dolls, guitars, and *sombreros!*

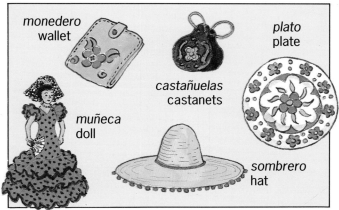

monedero
wallet

castañuelas
castanets

plato
plate

muñeca
doll

sombrero
hat

In a café

Cafés and bars are open all day long in Spain. People love to stop off for coffee or a cold drink, or just sit for a while and chat with a friend. Bar snacks called *tapas* are a real speciality — they can be anything from a few shrimps and olives, to a hot or cold mini-meal.

EATING TAPAS

If you order *tapas*, you'll be able to choose from dozens of dishes, depending on the part of Spain you're visiting. You may be able to try mussels, green peppers cooked in tomato, or even fried pig's ear!

Ice cream is called *helado*. Try *helado de fresa* (strawberry), *de pistacho*, or *de chocolate*.

FRUIT PUNCH

This cooling fruit drink is just right for hot summer days. As well as a big jug, you'll need:

1 apple, 1 orange
Strawberries
Lemonade
2 sprigs of mint
Lots of ice

1 Ask a grown-up to help you chop up the apple and strawberries and slice the orange.
2 Put everything in the jug, pouring in the lemonade last.
¡Salud! — cheers!

Eating and drinking

I n Spain, the main meal of the day is lunch. It is usually eaten late, at 2 or 3 P.M. A typical lunch often has three to four courses — as well as an appetizer and a dessert, there may be a fish dish and a meat course.

Supper is eaten at 9 or 10 P.M. This much simpler meal may be pasta or a *tortilla* — a potato omelette.

On special days, breakfast might be a glass of hot chocolate and crunchy *churros*.

Many Spanish dishes are cooked in olive oil. Olives are also eaten whole as a tasty snack.

Sandwiches are called *bocadillos*, and they're made with rolls or a chunk of crusty bread.

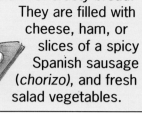

They are filled with cheese, ham, or slices of a spicy Spanish sausage (*chorizo*), and fresh salad vegetables.

Paella is one of Spain's most famous dishes. It is made from rice, seafood, and chicken, and its yellow color comes from a spice called saffron.

Each region of Spain has its own desserts. In Galicia in the northwest, they make an unusual rice pudding, browning the top with a red-hot poker.

Things to see and do

All over Spain there are amazing castles, built hundreds of years ago for kings and nobles. With more than 1,500 castles, there's bound to be one nearby for you to visit. Some castles are now in ruins. Others have been turned into museums or grand hotels.

△ South of Madrid, you can see the windmills made famous by the story of Don Quixote, a knight who challenged one of them to a duel!

◁ Guadamur Castle, near Toledo.

There are things to see in Spain that are even more ancient than its castles. The stone bulls of Guisando, near Avila, were carved thousands of years ago.

In the countryside

S ummers in southern Spain are
baking hot — perfect for olive trees.
Late in the year, the branches are
beaten to knock down the ripe olives.
Some are bottled or canned. Others are
crushed and squeezed into oil. Grapes
also thrive in Spain's sunny weather
and lots of good wine is made here.

DONKEY WORK

In some parts of Spain, people still use donkeys to help with farm work. The donkeys may be harnessed so that they can pull heavy carts or, like the one in this picture, they may carry baskets called panniers on their backs.

Grapes are picked in early fall, then pressed to make wine.

A visit to Madrid...

M adrid has been the capital of Spain for over 400 years. It has many fine buildings, museums, and art galleries such as the Prado. There are parks to walk in, too. At the city's heart is a huge square called the Plaza Mayor.

▽ Long ago, the Plaza Mayor was where Spanish kings and queens were crowned. It was also used for bullfights.

△ Not far from the Plaza Mayor is the Royal Palace. The king and queen don't live there, but they use it for important banquets.

...and Barcelona

The second biggest Spanish city is Barcelona, on the northeast coast. A famous tree-lined avenue called the Rambla leads from the harbor right into the city's heart. Packed with cafés and flower shops, the Rambla is a favorite place for an evening stroll, or *paseo*.

The Sagrada Familia is a fairy-tale cathedral, designed by Antonio Gaudí.

Traveling around

Spain is a large country and, after Switzerland, the most mountainous in Europe. Although smaller roads can be windy and slow, there is little traffic on them. Highways, called *autopistas*, are a fast route between big cities.

Taking a local bus is one of the best ways of exploring a town. You pay as you board. Madrid and Barcelona also have underground trains.

A CABLE CAR RIDE

If you visit Barcelona, you could take the cable car that runs right across the harbor all the way up to the top of Montjuïc – a mountain with museums and a park on top. You'll get a spectacular view over the city as you ride.

The most peaceful way to travel is on horseback, well away from cars and roads. The region of Andalucía in the south is famous for its beautiful horses, and riding vacations are always very popular here.

School and play

S chool in Spain lasts from 9 A.M. to 5 P.M., with an hour-and-a-half break for lunch. Summers are far too hot for sitting in a classroom, and vacation lasts from June to September. There's lots of time for enjoying outdoor games like *pelota*.

Pelota is said to be the world's fastest ball game and is very like jai alai which is played in the United States. It can be played against a wall, or in special courts. Each player has a curved basket to throw and catch the ball.

The most popular sport in Spain is probably soccer. Madrid and Barcelona both have world-famous soccer teams.

PLAY CHAPAS

Here's a game that schoolchildren play during recess. All you need are some metal bottle tops and a different colored paper for each player.

1 Cut out circles of paper to fit in your bottle tops and glue them inside.

2 Take turns flicking the tops against a wall. The player whose tops land closest to the wall wins, scooping up everyone else's.

Celebrations

Festivals are called *fiestas* in Spain and most cities, towns, and villages have their own special ones. Often a *fiesta* celebrates the birthday of a special saint or a famous person, with fireworks and carnivals. Sometimes people dress up in huge papier-mâché costumes. The celebrations usually carry on long into the night.

MAKE CASTANETS

You'll need wallpaper paste, cardboard, newspapers, black poster paint, clear varnish, and a ribbon.

1 Mix a bowl of paste. Cut out two cardboard castanet shapes.
2 Tear eight pages of paper into small strips. Dip them in paste and smooth them over the cards. Add several layers, leaving each one to dry, until you have the rounded shape shown below.
3 Make a hole in the top of each castanet.
4 Paint and varnish the castanets, then thread the ribbon through the holes to tie them together.

In the south, you may see women and men dancing the *flamenco*, stamping their feet and clicking castanets to guitar music.

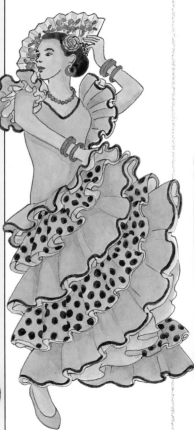

Let's Speak Spanish!

NUMBERS

1	Uno
2	Dos
3	Tres
4	Cuatro
5	Cinco
6	Seis
7	Siete
8	Ocho
9	Nueve
10	Diez

Buenos días
Hello

Por favor
Please

Gracias
Thank you

Quiero un helado, por favor.
I'd like some ice cream, please.
¿Cuánto cuesta éste?
How much is this one?

¿Habla inglés?
Do you speak English?

No
No

Sí
Yes

Index